SQUADRONS!

No. 49

AF437412

THE SUPERMARINE
SPITFIRE MK. I
THE BEGINNING
(THE AUXILIARY SQUADRONS)

PHIL H. LISTEMANN

ISBN: 979-1096490-82-0

Copyright

© **2021 Philedition - Phil Listemann**

updated Nov.2023

Colour profiles: Gaetan Marie/Bravo Bravo Aviation

PERSONEL :
(AUS)/RAF: Australian serving in the RAF
(BEL)/RAF: Belgian serving in the RAF
(CAN)/RAF: Canadian serving in the RAF
(CZ)/RAF: Czechoslovak serving in the RAF
(NFL)/RAF: Newfoundlander serving in the RAF
(NL)/RAF: Dutch serving in the RAF
(NZ)/RAF: New Zealander serving in the RAF
(POL)/RAF: Pole serving in the RAF
(RHO)/RAF: Rhodesian serving in the RAF
(SA)/RAF: South African serving in the RAF
(US)/RAF - RCAF : American serving in the RAF or RCAF

RANKS
G/C : Group Captain
W/C : Wing Commander
S/L : Squadron Leader
F/L : Flight Lieutenant
F/O : Flying Officer
P/O : Pilot Officer
W/O : Warrant Officer
F/Sgt : Flight Sergeant
Sgt : Sergeant
Cpl : Corporal
LAC : Leading Aircraftman

OTHER
ATA: Air Transport Auxiliary
CO : Commander
DFC : Distinguished Flying Cross
DFM : Distinguished Flying Medal
DSO : Distinguished Service Order
Eva. : Evaded
ORB : Operational Record Book
OTU : Operational Training Unit
PoW : Prisoner of War
PAF: Polish Air Force
RAF : Royal Air Force
RAAF : Royal Australian Air Force
RCAF : Royal Canadian Air Force
RNZAF : Royal New Zealand Air Force
SAAF : South African Air Force
s/d: Shot down
Sqn : Squadron
† : Killed

CODENAMES - OFFENSIVE OPERATIONS - FIGHTER COMMAND

CIRCUS:
Bombers heavily escorted by fighters, the purpose being to bring enemy fighters into combat.

RAMROD:
Bombers escorted by fighters, the primary aim being to destroy a target.

RANGER:
Large formation freelance intrusion over enemy territory with aim of wearing down enemy figthers.

RHUBARD:
Freelance fighter sortie against targets of opportunity.

RODEO:
A fighter sweep without bombers.

SWEEP:
An offensive flight by fighters designed to draw up and clear the enemy from the sky.

THE SPITFIRE MK. I

The Spitfire was the result of research carried out by its designer, Reginald J. Mitchell, an engineer with the Supermarine company. The latter had built up a solid reputation internationally in aviation competitions with its seaplanes from the S.4, which set a world speed record in its category in 1925, to the S.6B which won the Schneider Cup for Great Britain in 1931 and, shortly after, set a world record speed of 407.50 mph. Mitchell stood apart from other designers of the time as he went to great lengths to achieve a stream-lined profile for his designs. It was thanks to him that Supermarine built its reputation towards the end of the twenties, then strove to win contracts in order to ensure its survival, in the meantime getting by on subcontract work. Before the Spitfire, Mitchell tried to put forward a prototype fighter that met the F.7/30 programme (the Bristol Bulldog's replacement); this was eventually won by Gloster with a design that would become the Gladiator. Despite this failure, Mitchell carried on, outside of the official programme, with the study of a cantilever-winged monoplane, with an enclosed cockpit and retracting undercarriage, which he named the Type 300. The only thing that was missing was the ideal engine for this promising airframe. As luck would have it, at the same time, Rolls-Royce was working on a new, just as promising, project, the PV12, which was in its final development phase. The latter would go on to become the famous Merlin. Mitchell then had the idea of associating his airframe with this engine. At this point, no one knew this combination would go on to become one of the best fighters of the Second World War and arguably the most famous military aircraft of them all.

While the project was initially funded by company money, the British Air Ministry soon began to show an interest and finally decided to finance the design phase of the Spitfire via a new programme finalised on 3 January 1935, F.37/34. The prototype was ready a year later and, in the meantime, had been named 'Spitfire'. On 5 March 1936, Spitfire K5054, the first of a very long line, took off on its maiden flight. It was powered by a version of the Rolls-Royce PV12; the company had officially named this engine 'Merlin'. The 'C' version in K5054 only had a power output of 750hp but, despite this, the first trials were a success with the aircraft reaching a speed of 349 mph at an altitude of almost 20,000 feet. The trials continued and, on 3 June 1936, the first order for 310 aircraft was placed by the Air Ministry (**K9787–K9999, L1000–L1096**). Compared to the prototype, the production aircraft were fitted with a 1030hp Rolls-Royce Merlin II, exhaust pipes, radio equipment and a tail wheel, whereas the exterior protection flaps for the wheels were deleted. The armament consisted of the new standard of eight 0.303-in machine guns. However, the company was faced with numerous problems concerning the production of the elliptical wings and the set up was still not able to cope with the exigencies of mass production; thus, the production of a Spitfire required 30 per cent more man hours than the construction of a Hawker Hurricane. Delays began to increase, and the Air Ministry even considered not ordering more Spitfires, but the problems were ironed out and another order for 200 aircraft (**N3023–N3299**) was signed in September 1938 in the midst of the Munich crisis. This order was soon followed by several others: 200 in April 1939 (**P9305–P9567**), and 450 in August (**R6683–R7350**). Upon Great Britain's declaration of war, new orders soon began flooding in: 450 in March 1940, 500 at the beginning of June 1940, then 500 more in July, 300 in August and, finally, 1100 in October, making a total of more than 3000 aircraft. Although in many cases these Spitfires saw service as later versions, it is easy to see the space the Spitfire was beginning to occupy within the RAF. In all, 1556 Spitfires were built and delivered between August 1938 and December 1941. The last batches eventually built as Mk.Is belong to the order placed with serials **X4009–X4997** and **AR212–AR621**. When production of the Spitfire Mk.I was launched, several improvements were added to the production aircraft. Among the most notable of these was that, from the 75th airframe,

A view of the port side of the prototype, K5054.

K5054 after its landing accident on 15.03.1938 at Martlesham Heath. The aircraft was repaired but was destroyed in a flying accident at Farnborough the day after the declaration of the war.

the Merlin III replaced the Merlin II; this allowed for both the three-blade de Havilland or Rotol propellers to be fitted while retaining power output. The 78th aircraft to roll off the production line saw the definitive adoption of the three-blade propeller in place of the two-blade version. Of course, with what was learnt from the first combat reports, improvements were made to the Spitfire throughout 1940 and 1941. However, the most virulent criticism concerned the armament and, in mid-1940, the RAF sought to improve it. Already, in June 1939, trials had been undertaken with the mounting of a 20mm cannon in each wing. Although this weapon proved to be unreliable in certain combat phases, the decision was made to arm a few Spitfire Mk.Is and use them operationally. The aircraft thus armed were designated as Mk.IB, which meant the Air Ministry had to retroactively rename those Spitfires armed with eight machine guns as Mk.IAs. Thirty Mk.IBs were produced, little by little, though, as the Hispano-Suiza cannons were only available in small numbers; the first examples were armed with four cannons and the others with two cannons and four machine guns. Deployed with No. 19 Squadron, the unreliability of the cannons was evident and the authorities had to find a compromise solution, with the mixed installation of cannons/machine guns, in order to prevent the Spitfire from being without armament in the course of a dogfight. This initial flaw turned out to be beneficial as, a few months later, when the problem concerning reliability was solved, this mixed armament became standard for the Spitfire and would remain so for several years.

In the meantime, the Spitfire had attracted the attention of foreign countries and, upon the declaration of war in September 1939, a dozen had come forward with orders or seeking permission to build the type under licence. The number of probable orders was between 190 and 292 aircraft. Thus, we can reasonably declare that, compared to other European fighters of this time, the Spitfire would have, beyond doubt, been a very successful export if war had not got in the way. However, paradoxically, the Spitfire Mk.I was only exported in small numbers – eighteen for Portugal and three for Turkey. The Spitfire Mk.I was the version that suffered the most in the initial fighting, especially during the hard-fought Battle of Britain. When the last Mk.I was delivered to the RAF, there were only 450 left in the inventory, less than a third of what was built. It is true that four had been converted into Mk.IIs and another 168 into Mk.Vs, especially in 1941 (plus a few reconnaissance conversions), but the 450 reveals the tough fighting of the first two years of the war during which pilots flying the Spitfire Mk.I claimed almost 2000 confirmed or probable kills, many during the Battle of Britain.

In 1941–42, the Mk.I was beginning to be used mainly for fighter pilot training, mostly within OTUs (Operational Training Units). In concrete terms, it was retired from front-line units in mid-1941 and replaced by later types, particularly the Mk.V. Continuing in the thankless role of a training machine, the number of Mk.Is gradually dwindled; on 31 December 1944, less than seventy were still present in the inventory, but they were worn out. The end of the war was on the horizon, and the RAF had plenty of later Spitfires in its depots, so it decided to cease using the Mk.I; the variant was finally declared obsolete in February 1945. It should also be noted that, from 1943 onwards, 77 Mk.Is were leased to the Fleet Air Arm (FAA) as training aircraft following the arrival of the Seafire in the ranks of the FAA. The surviving airframes were returned to the RAF in the final months of the war and immediately retired from service.

Until the beginning of the Battle of Britain, the RAF had nineteen operational fighter squadrons, of which six were Auxiliary Air Force (AAF) units called to operational duties on the eve of the outbreak of war (602, 603, 609, 610, 611 and 616). Initially, this separate branch of the RAF had been formed to provide a reserve of an elite corps of civilians who flew in their spare time. Those squadrons received a new number plate range starting with 600. The pilots of the AAF were generally from the wealthier classes, as applicants were expected to already have, or be prepared to obtain at their own expense, their pilot's licence. Pilots of the AAF were expected to join for a period of no less than five years and were required to fly a few hours every quarter and attend annual training for fifteen days.

At the outbreak of war, the AAF squadrons were brought under the RAF and received reinforcements to reach operational status. Pilots coming from regular RAF squadrons were posted in and progressively these AAF units became fighter squadrons like any other in the RAF. However, until the Battle of Britain, the majority of the pilots serving in the squadrons were from the pre-war AAF.

Above, Spitfire P9450 during a test flight in April 1940 before delivery to the RAF. This Spitfire belonged to a batch more suitable for combat than previous examples, especially the ones that fought during the initial stages of the war. This specific aircraft was issued to an operational unit in early June 1940.

Left, Spitfire L1007 was the first Spitfire fitted with the twin 20mm Hispano cannon arrangement. The mods were completed in June 1939 with operational testing being carried out from autumn 1939.

Victories - confirmed or probable claims: 4.25

First operational sortie: 08.09.39
Last operational sortie: 30.06.40

Number of sorties: *ca.* 1,300
Total aircraft written-off: 7

Aircraft lost on operations: 5
Aircraft lost in accidents: 2

Squadron code letters:
LO

COMMANDING OFFICERS

| S/L Andrew D. FARQUHAR | AAF No. 90158 | RAF | ... | 04.04.40 |
| S/L George C. PINKERTON | AAF No. 90160 | RAF | 04.04.40 | ... |

SQUADRON USAGE

As with other Auxiliary units, No. 602 Squadron began its existence as a bomber unit. Its role changed twice, first, in 1938, to army-cooperation, then, in January 1939, to fighters. It was based at Abbotsinch in Scotland and replaced its Hawker Hectors with Gloster Gauntlets. These were used to work-up on fighter tactics before Spitfires arrived in May (the first Auxiliary unit to fly the new type). It became part of No. 13 Group in July and was deemed operational by 28 August. By that time the squadron was com-

manded by S/L A.D. Farquhar. Training was intensified once war was declared and more pilots reached the squadron. By the 7th, 602 had 23 on strength. The next day, the squadron experienced its first war fatality when Sgt J.M. C. Bryden took-off at 22:10 on his first night flight in a Spitfire. He was seen heading off into the darkness, banking at about 500 feet, and then the Spitfire dived at full throttle into the ground, creating a fireball visible for miles around. It was not a good day for 602 as another Spitfire was badly damaged by Sgt A. McDowall, also on his first night flight on the type, but, on the positive side, the unit also carried out its first operational sorties when Blue Section of B Flight was ordered to patrol Turnhouse at 3000 feet. On proceeding there, orders were received to head to Gullane to intercept an enemy aircraft but, after patrolling for seven minutes, the section was ordered to return home. Three weeks later, three sections were ordered to patrol; Flight Lieutenant A.V. R.

Andrew Farquhar joined 602 Sqn in 1927, assumed command ten years later and was still in the role when war broke out. He led 602 during the first weeks of the war and, after his first successes, was awarded the DFC in March 1940 and posted to command Martlesham Heath. Despite his rank and station command responsibilities, he flew ops during the Battle of Britain and made several more claims. He eventually returned to an official operational role in March 1941 when he became the Hornchurch Wing Leader, a position he held until June. This was his last operational posting. He was released from the RAF in 1945.

A line-up of 602 Sqn Spitfires shortly after the declaration of war. The former peace-time codes 'ZT' have been changed to 'LO'. In the foreground, K9970 was 'LO-D' at the time.

'Sandy' Johnstone was off the ground at 02:28 but, with a complete black-out over the Glasgow area, he was unable to find his bearings or intercept the unidentified aircraft. Now in an uncomfortable situation, he decided to make a forced landing; he released a parachute flare so he was able to see the ground immediately beneath him. Things went wrong and the landing became a crash from which Johnstone escaped without injury. Another similar action took place on 1 October with one aircraft but, again, no interception was made. On 6 October, 602 moved to its war station at Grangemouth, then to Drem on the 13th from which its first operational convoy patrols were flown. This move proved a wise one. A few days after the squadron's arrival, the Luftwaffe made its first attack on British soil when a force of He111s attacked naval ships in the Forth; in conjunction with No. 603 Squadron, 602 was called to action. The squadrons shared the honour of destroying the first enemy aircraft of the war over Britain. October 16 started with relatively good weather for the time of year and 6–7/10 broken cloud. At 09:20, the Chain Home RDF station at Drone Hill near Coldingham detected two intruders over the North Sea. These were Heinkel He 111s of *Kampfgeschwader* 26 (KG26), based at Westerland on Sylt, Germany, at that time the nearest Luftwaffe base to Britain. The Heinkels were fitted with cameras and they carried out tactical reconnaissance sorties. The German crews knew Spitfires were based near the Firth of Forth. After being detected by RDF, at 09:45, Royal Observer Corps' reports placed one unidentified aircraft at high altitude on a south-westerly course over Dunfermline heading for Rosyth, with another flying across the Borders near Galashiels. Three minutes later, at 09:48, Blue Section of 602 Squadron (three Spitfires led by F/L G. Pinkerton) was scrambled to patrol the Island of May at 5000 feet. At 10:08, one He111 was spotted by lookouts on board the cruiser HMS *Edinburgh* at anchor in the estuary. Shortly afterwards, the bomber was observed over Drem. Blue Section patrolled over the Island of May for twenty minutes before being ordered by the Turnhouse operations room to move south towards Dunbar. Pinkerton spotted the Heinkel and at 10:21 ordered his section into line astern to make

The wreckage of Heinkel He111H '1H+JA', of Stab KG26, shot down on 28.10.39 by Nos 602 and 603 Squadrons (partially credited to future Battle of Britain ace F/O A. A. 'Archie' McKellar).
(Andrew Thomas)

an attack on the enemy bomber. However, the Germans made a sharp turn to the left to escape into clouds. Still some distance away, Pinkerton fired at the fleeing enemy aircraft, as did one of his pilots, F/O A.A. McKellar, apparently doing no damage or, at least, nothing conclusive. Over the course of the rest of the morning, Spitfires from 602 Squadron continued to be scrambled to try, unsuccessfully, to intercept unknown intruders. The day, however, was not over. Advised on the weather and possible naval targets by the returning Heinkels, twelve Junkers Ju88s from KG30 in four groups of three took off that afternoon. At 14:20, the Observer Corps reported enemy aircraft over East Lothian and, shortly afterwards, Turnhouse ordered 602 Squadron's Blue Section (Pinkerton, McKellar and P.C. Webb) to scramble from Drem to investigate two unidentified aircraft over Tranent. They were joined by 603 Squadron and both squadrons intercepted the enemy raid on shipping in the Forth. Blue Section arrived while a group of Ju88s was heading for home. Pinkerton and McKellar spotted a lone Ju88 heading for the North Sea, pursued it and managed to damage it so badly the pilot had to ditch his aircraft into the sea (the claim was made for an He111). There were still more Ju88s approaching but no further claims were made as far as 602 was concerned. It was a busy day for the squadron with thirty sorties flown. The Luftwaffe returned on the 28th leading to another interception by both 602 and 603 Squadrons with one He111 from KG26 shared between the two squadrons; the lucky pilot from 602 was McKellar. Pinkerton was awarded the DFC the following month for his actions on the day. The Heinkel came down substantially intact and was the first enemy aircraft to be brought down on British soil since WWI. Routine patrols were flown in November and December, but the Luftwaffe did not show up. Sadly, 602 shot down two No. 44 Squadron Hampdens by mistake; the bombers were returning from a raid and one crew member was killed. The subsequent court of inquiry cleared the fighter squadron of blame. During this period, 602 wrecked three Spitfires, the first two when K9974, flown by F/O N. Stone, ran into L1079 after it overshot the runway. Both aircraft were later written off. On 30 December, while practising aerobatics, nineteen year old Sgt B.P. Bailey was killed after a wingtip touched the ground.

Patrols continued in the first weeks of 1940. On 13 January, a Heinkel 111 was intercepted and Red Section, led by F/L M. Robinson, managed to damage it before it was shot down by Hurricanes from No. 111 Squadron; the Heinkel was seen to go into the sea about fifteen miles east of Carnoustie. Despite the initial damage caused by 602, full credit went to 111 Squadron. The unit was more effective on 9 February when S/L Farquhar, flying with F/O A.M; Grant engaged an He111 about twenty miles out to sea. The Heinkel, from II./KG26, was on a recce mission when it was intercepted. Only Farquhar opened fire and after having expended 625 rounds of ammunition, the Spitfire mortally wounded the wireless operator, who was manning the top gun position, and damaged the oil sumps and radiators of both engines. The German pilot was obliged to make a forced landing at North Berwick with the undercarriage down; both tyres were punctured and the aircraft ran into a hedge, tipping up onto its nose. Three of the four crewmen survived and were interned as PoWs. This aircraft was not that damaged and became a very useful war trophy as it was repaired and evaluated, later becoming AW177 and flying with No. 1426 (Enemy Aircraft) Flight. Unfortunately, it was involved in a fatal accident on 10 November 1943, causing the death of seven people. Farquhar received the DFC four days later for this action. Aside from these victories, 602 began to test cannon-equipped Spitfires, P/O G.V. Proudman, attached from 65 Squadron with Spitfire L1007, performing three cannon tests at sea during the month. Two weeks later, P/O Proudman had the opportunity to use the cannons on a German aircraft. On 22 February, S/L Farquhar, P/O G.V. Proudman (the latter flying L1007) and F/O C.H. MacLean engaged an

Pilots of 602 Sqn at the beginning of 1940:
Standing, left to right: F/O W. H. Coverley (†07.09.40), F/L P. C. Webb, F/O D. McF. Jack, W/O C. L. McIntosh (groundcrew), Flying Officers A. M. Grant and A. A. McKellar (†01.11.40 with 605 Sqn), and P/O T. G. F. Ritchie (†21.07.41)
Seated, left to right: Flight Lieutenants J. D. Urie and M. Robinson, S/L A. D. Farquhar (CO), and Flight Lieutenants A. V. R. Johnstone and R. F. Boyd.

The Heinkel He111 of 5./KG26 coded 1H+EN shot down by S/L A. D. Farquhar on 9 February 1940. The aircraft was repaired and flown by the RAF as AW177.
(Andrew Thomas)

He111 about twenty miles out to sea. The Heinkel from 1.(F)/Aufkl.Gr. ObdL was on a recce mission when it was intercepted and the combat was engaged. Proudman fired 64 cannon shells, 60 from one gun and four from the other one before it jammed. He definitively saw his high explosive rounds exploding on the right mainplane between the fuselage and just outside the engine. The German pilot was forced to crash the Heinkel and the crew then set fire to the aircraft at Lumsdaine near St-Abbs Head. Farquhar tried to land next to the Heinkel to prevent its destruction but, due to wet ground, he overturned and had to be rescued by the enemy crew! He didn't manage to save the Heinkel from destruction himself, but almost lost a precious Spitfire (it was repaired, Farquhar avoided getting into too much trouble as a result). The He111 was carrying two incendiary bombs, principally for destroying the aircraft, and the crew was ready to activate them but were prevented from doing so by the police, although one of the crew dropped a cigarette end into a pool of leaking petrol that did not ignite. Farquhar and Proudman shared credit for shooting down the Heinkel as MacLean did not open fire as he had turned back fearing an engine failure. On 2 March, he was involved in an accident when he got lost during a night patrol, ran out of fuel and made a forced landing at Dunbar. March also saw Farquhar's promotion to wing commander on the 13th; he continued to lead 602 until 4 April when S/L Pinkerton returned to take command. Farquhar then left to command Martlesham Heath. April was otherwise quiet except that the squadron split on the 14th, A Flight moving to Montrose and B Flight to Dyce. This situation lasted until 28 May when 602 returned to Drem and, in the weeks to the end of June, flew ninety patrols. In the meantime, the Germans had launched their offensive to the west, but this did not bring any major changes for the pilots of 602 Squadron. It was routine as usual even though some accidents did occur. A pilot of No. 74 Squadron taxied his Spitfire into N3165, badly damaging it to the point that it was struck off charge on 14 June. The squadron didn't participate in the evacuation of Dunkirk and continued its routine tasks from Drem until the end of June. On the 15th, all of the unit's Spitfires received new undersurface paint with Duck Egg Blue being introduced. In the early hours of 26 June, Turnhouse was bombed by German intruders. Flight Lieutenant Johnstone got permission to take-off and patrol base. After thirty minutes, he was ordered to look for a possible enemy aircraft approaching his position and soon saw an He111, emerging from a cloud at 6000 feet, illuminated by searchlights. He called up Control and reported he was going into attack. He approached his target from astern and to the right, noticing slight amounts of smoke coming from the bomber's right engine. Johnstone opened fire from 200 yards but, owing to his fast overtaking speed, he only got in a short burst of about three seconds before he had to pull up to avoid a collision. He came round again and delivered an attack from astern and below. This time, large volumes of smoke began to issue from both engines as he got in a burst of six seconds. The Heinkel was still well illuminated by searchlights. It was now rapidly losing height and he followed it down in the direction of Dunbar. As the He111 was now leaving the searchlight area, Johnstone delivered a third attack from astern to make sure of its destruction. He fired a burst of about four seconds and followed it down until it hit the water about ten miles south-east of Dunbar.

The last few days of June were uneventful for the squadron. The month ended with two night patrols carried out by F/L R.F. Boyd and F/O W.H. Coverley between 23:40 and 01:15 on 30 June/1 July.

Its engine warming up, Spitfire K9964/LO-B, christened 'Bogus', is about to taxi out for another patrol.

Claims - 602 Squadron (Confirmed and Probable)

Date	Pilot	SN	Origin	Type	Serial	Code	Nb	Cat.
16.10.39	F/L George C. **Pinkerton**	AAF No. 90160	RAF	He111			0.50	C
	F/L Archibald A. **McKellar**	AAF No. 90168	RAF		**K9979**		0.50	C
28.10.39	F/L Archibald A. **McKellar** *shared with 603 Sqn*	AAF No. 90168	RAF	He111	**K9977**	LO-P	0.25	C
09.02.40	S/L Andrew D. **Furquhar**	AAF No. 90158	RAF	He111	**K9962**	LO-A	1.0	C
22.02.40	S/L Andrew D. **Furquhar**	AAF No. 90158	RAF	He111	**K9962**	LO-A	0.50	C
	P/O George V. **Proudman**	RAF No. 39947	RAF		**L1007***		0.50	C
26.06.40	F/L Alexander V.R. **Johnstone**	AAF No. 90163	RAF	He111 [1]	**L1004**	LO-Q	1.0	C

Total: 4.25

*cannon equipped.

[1] by night

Some 602 Sqn pilots began to shine before the Battle of Britain. Among them were Flight Lieutenants 'Sandy' Johnstone (left) and 'Archie' McKellar (right). Serving with 602 before the war, McKellar was called to full-time service as hostilities commenced. His first successes and leadership skills saw him posted as a flight commander to 605 Sqn at the end of June 1940, flying Hurricanes, where he saw out the Battle of Britain. In action throughout the summer and autumn of 1940, he achieved considerable success, making more than 26 claims. A DFC was awarded in September and a Bar followed three weeks later, by which time he had assumed command of the squadron. He was killed on 1 November trying to make a forced landing in his damaged Hurricane near Adisham after combat with Bf109 fighter-bombers. He was made a Companion of the DSO two weeks later. He is credited with twenty destroyed (three shared), five probables and three damaged. 'Sandy' Johnstone was also serving with 602 before the war. He stayed with the squadron during the Battle of Britain and eventually led it in mid-July. He increased his score and a DFC was awarded in October; his score at the time was nine destroyed (two shared), one probable and seven damaged. He left 602 in mid-April 1941 and was posted to the Middle East the following autumn. After various non-operational positions, he returned for a second tour in January 1943 as Krendi Wing Leader on Malta. This was a brief posting as he was back in the UK in March. No further operational positions were held before the end of the war. He remained in the RAF and retired in 1968 as an Air Vice-Marshal.

Summary of the aircraft lost on Operations - 602 Squadron

Date	Pilot	S/N	Origin	Serial	Code	Fate
01.10.39	F/L Alexander V.R. **JOHNSTONE**	AAF No. 90163	RAF	**K9973**	LO-Q	-
02.03.40	P/O George V. **PROUDMAN***	RAF No. 39947	RAF	**K9978**	LO-G	-

Total: 2

*Attached from 65 Sqn

Date	Pilot	S/N	Origin	Serial	Code	Fate
08.09.39	Sgt John M.C. **BRYDEN**	AAF No. 802600	RAF	**K9965**		†
26.11.39	P/O Norman **STONE**	AAF No. 90172	RAF	**K9974**	LO-H	-
	Destroyed on ground collision			**L1079**		-
30.12.39	Sgt Brian P. **BAILEY**	RAF No. 741799	RAF	**K9977**	LO-P	†
27.05.40	*Ground accident*	-	-	**N3165**		-

Total: 5

Two views of K9899/LO-H at Drem during the first days of June 1940. New markings have begun to be introduced with the new fin flash and fuselage roundels evident. However, this Spitfire is still wearing the topside wing roundels which were quite common at the beginning of the war. K9899 was issued to 602 Sqn at the end of March 1940. In June, it was the regular mount of F/O A. M. Grant before he left on the 23rd for operational duties at Pembrey.

between **September 1939 &**
June 1940

Victories - confirmed or probable claims: 4.75

First operational sortie:	**Number of sorties:** *n/k*
16.10.39	
Last operational sortie:	**Total aircraft written-off: 9**
30.06.40	

Aircraft lost on operations: 5
Aircraft lost in accidents: 4

Squadron code letters:
XT

COMMANDING OFFICERS

S/L Ernest H. Stevens	AAF No. 90182	RAF	...	05.06.40
S/L George L. Denholm	AAF No. 90190	RAF	05.06.40	...

SQUADRON USAGE

This unit was originally formed at Turnhouse as a light bomber squadron during the interwar period. It became a fighter squadron in October 1938 and received some Gloster Gladiators. At the time, 603 was under the command of S/L E.H. Stevens. War was declared and, two weeks later, the first Spitfire arrived, on the 14th, followed by seven others the next day. Conversion to the new mount began at once and continued for several weeks. In the meantime, the squadron received a full complement of aircraft with the arrival of one Spitfire on 21 September and three more the following day. Sadly, on 1 October, F/O J.A.B. Somerville was killed in L1047 while taxiing when Spitfire L1059, flown by P/O J.S. Morton, collided with him on landing after a night patrol. A week later, another accident occurred; the pilot, P/O G.C. Hunter, was seriously injured when he crashed on the edge of the runway when approaching to land in hazy conditions. At that time, the squadron was still training on the Spitfires while the few operational patrols were carried out by the remaining Gladiators. On 16 October, there was a raid on naval vessels in the Firth of Forth for which the squadron scrambled six Spitfires at 14:30; Red Section was led by F/L P. Gifford and Yellow Section by F/L G.L. Denholm. Yellow

The 'RL' codes were used by 603 Sqn before the war. They were changed to 'XT' upon the outbreak of war and retained while the squadron was in the UK. Here, L1050/XT-H is seen at Turnhouse during the autumn of 1939.

Pilots of 603 Sqn in March 1940:
Standing, left to right: Sgt J. R. Caister (POW 06.09.40), Flying Officers I. S. Ritchie and J. S. Morton, Pilot Officers G. K. Gilroy and A. Barton (IO), and W/O J. Dalziel (groundcrew). Seated, left to right: F/O J. G. E. Haig, F/L G. L. Denholm (became the CO in June), S/L E. H. Stevens (CO), and Flying Officers H. K. MacDonald (†28.09.40) and A. Wallace (Adj).
After participating in the Battle of Britain with the squadron, followed by a period of rest, George Denholm switched to a night fighting role flying Turbinlite Havocs. He later commanded 605 Sqn in the intruder role between August 1942 and May 1943.

Section engaged three bombers but these broke formation and fled into cloud, one of the German rear gunners managing to put a bullet into George Gilroy's Spitfire (L1048). Gifford's Section attacked a bomber too and the He111 (actually a Ju88 from I./KG 30) was seen to fall into the sea off Port Seton. Three of the four crewman were picked up and taken prisoner. An hour later, two Spitfires intercepted an He111 and chased it at low level out to sea. The Heinkel managed to escape with a dead engine and the rear gunner no longer firing. The squadron's pilots fired 16,000 rounds of ammunition across the entire day. More prevention patrols were flown that day, but nothing else happened. One week later, Red Section was again called to intercept a lone aircraft, a reconnaissance Heinkel 111 reported off St Abb's Head over a convoy. The three British pilots soon saw the raider and gave chase as it headed out to sea. They managed to catch it and, after an exchange of fire, it turned back towards the coast, apparently to try to force-land, but it came down in the sea seven miles out. Three members of the crew were seen to get into a dinghy and were later picked up by a Royal Navy destroyer. Two of the three Spitfires returned sporting bullet holes, but the damage was not serious. October proved to be very busy as, a few days later, on the 28th, Red Section was sent at 09:15 to intercept a raider; a section from 602 Squadron followed at 10:20. The bomber, an He111 from Stab/KG 26, was soon attacked, first by 602 and then by 603, and was eventually badly hit. After circling at low level, it made a good crash-landing in open country near Kidlaw, six miles south of Haddington. Two of the crew were killed and the pilot wounded; the remaining crewmember escaped injury. The three Spitfires fired 5600 rounds between them and the claim was shared by the two squadrons. The squadron subsequently returned to its routine and, in November, very few patrols were flown, the days mostly consumed with training. On the administrative side, Gifford, for his actions in October, received the DFC, one of the first for the Fighter Command. On 7 December, another combat took place. Blue Section (F/O J.L.G. Cunningham) was on patrol when it was warned of seven hostile aircraft approaching south-east of Montrose; No. 72 Squadron was also part of the game that day. Both squadrons found the bombers and Blue Section attacked some of them, claiming three as damaged (one per pilot, the other two men being P/O B.J.G. Carbury, a New Zealander, and Sgt R. Berry). It would be not until 19 January that any further encounters occurred with a single reconnaissance He111 approaching the coast of Scotland. The Heinkel was initially attacked by Sgt J.R. Caister who, flying alone on a shipping patrol when the approach of the intruder was reported, had set off at once to intercept, catching the Heinkel off Aberdeen at 12:05. He opened fire but, due to the extreme cold, several of his guns failed to operate. Soon after, Red Section (F/O J.G.E. Haig, F/O H.K. MacDonald and F/O C.H. MacLean) scrambled and eventually caught the bomber twenty miles east of Aberdeen. The Heinkel was easy to spot, the attack was launched from the quarter, and the pilots continued to fire until their guns stopped, not because they had run them dry but because most of their guns had frozen up. However, they saw the Heinkel's undercarriage drop and smoke pour from the aircraft but observed no definite results. In fact, the bomber continued to descend as it tried to reach home, finally crashing into sea;

two bodies were later recovered and the claim confirmed. Another interception attempt was made on 9 February but failed. The Heinkel was sighted and attacked by Green section (F/O Cunningham, F/O R. McG. Waterson and P/O B.G. Stapleton). Waterson managed to expend 800 rounds of ammunition, but no results were observed. Besides those interceptions, January and February consisted of uneventful patrols. March resembled the two previous months expect on 17 March when an enemy aircraft was spotted off Peterhead and Aberdeen (believed to be a Ju88) and intercepted by F/L Denholm and his section. Denholm fired a two-second burst before the enemy aircraft disappeared, while another aircraft (possibly a Do17) was intercepted five minutes later but disappeared in clouds after Red 3 (F/O Haig) had fired a four-second burst at it. There were no claims in March but there were several losses. Returning from a patrol on the 20th, F/O J.C. Boulter wrecked his Spitfire while landing when he collided with a stationary Airspeed Oxford on Montrose aerodrome; he was injured and sealed the fate of the Spitfire. It was the continuation of a bad run as, the previous day, the squadron mourned the death of one of its own when P/O G.I. Thomson was killed due to an error of judgment in poor visibility during a standing shipping patrol. March also saw P/O G.K. Gilroy escape injury after crashing during take-off from Dyce when he hit an Avro Anson (also taking off) on the 25th. In April, there was not much to report besides P/O W.A. Douglas crashing K9956 on the 17th. Attempting to land in a rainstorm while ferrying the aircraft from Montrose to Drem, he came down in a ploughed field close to the latter. The undercarriage of the Spitfire dug into the soil and the aircraft nosed-over onto its back; Douglas escaped unhurt. A few days later, P/O Stapleton's turn. A South African serving in the RAF, he had to bale out of his aircraft after damaging its undercarriage during a night landing. May was totally uneventful if we ignore the fact that all leaves were cancelled after the 10th when the Phoney War finally ended and the invasion of France, Belgium and the Low Countries commenced. It was business as usual with fighting patrols and training until the end of June. Major changes did take place that month, however. First of all, S/L Stevens was appointed as one of three controllers at Turnhouse as well as nominally being CO of 603. On 5 June, he was posted 'supernumerary non-effective sick' owing to ongoing medical problems and F/L Denholm was promoted to squadron leader and took command. Two more Spitfires were wrecked in June: N3244 on the 5th, Stapleton again escaping unhurt (the aircraft was eventually repaired), and L1050 on the 12th. This time, however, the pilot, F/O D.K. A. Mackenzie, was killed when, during a night training flight, he apparently became disoriented by a battery of searchlights. The ORB does not give details about operations; therefore, it is impossible to know how many patrols were flown during this period.

At the end of June, the British Isles began to receive regular visits from German bombers. On 26 June, Turnhouse was bombed for the first time. Flight Lieutenant MacDonald was initially guided to an enemy aircraft's position by a cluster of searchlights and then by anti-aircraft fire. He approached the from below and to one side. The aircraft turned left through 90° very gradually and he overhauled it before firing a solid burst of ten seconds from dead astern and slightly below, closing until he overshot and had to break away above as the bomber had started a spiral dive emitting sparks and smoke. When the alarm was first raised, F/O Haig was already airborne and may have shared in the destruction of a He111 but missed his chance. With his fuel running low, Haig requested permission to land at Turnhouse, 603 (City of Edinburgh) Squadron's base. This was refused; because of the possibility of German intruders still being in the area, the flare path was not switched on. Haig therefore turned away to open country; shortly afterwards his engine failed and, as it was too dark to attempt a forced landing, he baled out, spraining an ankle on landing while his Spitfire crashed south of Balerno. Haig was taken back to Turnhouse by a farmer in his lorry, not having convinced the latter that he wasn't a German. Two weeks later, the Battle of Britain officially began.

A line-up of 603 Sqn Spitfires with L1007/XT-K in the foreground.

Date	Pilot	SN	Origin	Type	Serial	Code	Nb	Cat.
16.10.39	F/L Patrick **GIFFORD**	AAF No. 90188	RAF	He111*	**L1070**	XT-A	0.33	C
	P/O Colin **ROBERTSON**	RAF No. 33412	RAF		**L1050**	XT-H	0.33	C
	F/O Harold K. **MacDONALD**	AAF No. 90193	RAF		**L1061**	XT-B	0.33	C
22.10.39	F/L Patrick **GIFFORD**	AAF No. 90188	RAF	He111	**L1070**	XT-A	0.33	C
	P/O Colin **ROBERTSON**	RAF No. 33412	RAF		**L1050**	XT-H	0.33	C
	P/O James S. **MORTON**	AAF No. 90727	RAF		**L1049**		0.33	C
28.10.39	F/L Patrick **GIFFORD**	AAF No. 90188	RAF	He111	**L1070**	XT-A	0.25	C
	P/O Colin **ROBERTSON**	RAF No. 33412	RAF		**L1050**	XT-H	0.25	C
	P/O George K. **GILROY** *shared with 602 Sqn*	AAF No. 90481	RAF		**L1049**		0.25	C
19.01.40	F/O Harold K. **MacDONALD**	AAF No. 90193	RAF	He111	**K9995**		0.33	C
	F/O John G. E. **HAIG**	AAF No. 90189	RAF		**L1048**		0.33	C
	P/O George K. **GILROY**	AAF No. 90481	RAF		**L1057**	XT-X	0.33	C
26.06.40	F/O Harold K. **MacDONALD**	AAF No. 90193	RAF	He111 [1]			1.0	C

Total: 4.75

*Actually a Ju88

[1] by night

Among the pilots who opened their scores with 603 Sqn during the initial phase of the war was P/O 'Sheep' Gilroy. A Scot, he joined the Auxiliary Air Force with 603 before the war and was called to active service in August 1939. He participated in the Battle of Britain with 603, during which he increased his tally, but was shot down by Bf109s on 1 September. Injured, he nevertheless returned to combat with 603 before the end of the Battle of Britain, being awarded the DFC in the meantime. After another accident in December 1940, which took him off flying for two months, he was back with 603 by the end of February 1941. In July, he was given command of 609 Sqn and led the unit until the end of his tour in May 1942. A Bar to his DFC followed.

In November 1942, he was posted to North Africa to take over a wing leader position with 324 Wing. He was made a Companion of the DSO at the end of the Tunisian campaign. During his stay in North Africa, more successes were recorded and his last claim was made on 4 September 1943 to bring his score to 24 confirmed victories (ten shared), two shared probables and nine damaged. Two months later, he returned to the UK as a Group Captain, but no further operational positions were forthcoming before the end of the war.

Date	Pilot	S/N	Origin	Serial	Code	Fate
01.10.39	F/O James A. B. **Somerville**	AAF No. 90196	RAF	**L1047**		†
19.03.40	P/O Gordon I. **Thomson**	RAF No. 70878	RAF	**L1026**		†
20.03.40	F/O John C. **Boulter**	RAF No. 37757	RAF	**L1022**	XT-D	-
25.03.40	P/O George K. **Gilroy**	AAF No. 90481	RAF	**K9926**		-
26.06.40	F/O John G. E. **Haig**	AAF No. 90189	RAF	**N3190**		-

Total: 5

Two pilots serving with 603 Sqn during the Phoney War: Left, Bill Douglas joined 603 in March 1940. However, just before the Germans launched their offensive in May, he was posted out as a pilot to second-line units. It was not until September that he was posted to a front-line unit, joining 610 Sqn, later serving with 603 again and becoming a flight commander. He stayed with 603 when it was sent to Malta and, in July 1942, he took command of the squadron before it disbanded two weeks later. He was then given command of a newly reformed unit, 229 Sqn (also on Malta). On a second tour of ops, he took command of 611 Sqn where he made his final claims, bringing his total to six confirmed victories, three probables (one shared) and seven damaged. He ended the war with a DFC and Bar. Right, Basil Stapleton was a South African serving in the RAF. He was posted to 603 in December 1939 from 32 Sqn. He participated in the Battle of Britain with 603, making all of his claims with the unit – eight confirmed victories (two shared), eight probables and two damaged. Later in the war, he commanded 611 Sqn and then 247 Sqn. It was while leading 247 that he was shot down and made a POW on 23.12.44. He was a DFC recipient.

Date	Pilot	S/N	Origin	Serial	Code	Fate
07.10.39	P/O Graham C. **Hunter**	AAF No. 90474	RAF	**L1023**		-
17.04.40	P/O William A. **Douglas**	AAF No. 90896	RAF	**K9956**	XT-P	-
26.04.40	P/O Basil G. **Stapleton**	RAF No. 41879	(SA)/RAF	**L1025**		-
12.06.40	P/O Donald K.A. **Mackenzie**	AAF No. 90861	RAF	**L1050**	XT-H	†

Total: 4

Victories - confirmed or probable claims: 9.0

First operational sortie:
14.10.39
Last operational sortie:
30.06.40

Number of sorties: *ca.* 1,300

Total aircraft written-off: 10

Aircraft lost on operations: 6
Aircraft lost in accidents: 4

Squadron code letters:
PR

COMMANDING OFFICERS

S/L Geoffrey H. AMBER	AAF No. 90296	RAF	...	28.12.39
S/L Mark T. AVENT	AAF No. 90242	RAF	28.12.39	28.06.40
S/L Horace S. DARLEY	RAF No. 32191	RAF	28.06.40	...

SQUADRON USAGE

Formed in February 1936, 609 Squadron was initially a light bomber unit. It became a fighter squadron in December 1938 but, by the outbreak of war, it only had two Spitfires and a Fairey Battle on hand. Based at Yeadon, West Yorkshire, when the war began, it moved to Catterick. The Officer Commanding was S/L G.H. Ambler. On 3 September, 609 received a batch of Spitfires (L1081 to L1088). Three days later, more were collected (L1058, L1060, L1065 and L1071). Training intensified and the first incident occurred on the 7th when F/O E.R. Edge made a gear-up landing, fortunately without serious consequences for the pilot or the aircraft. Building up to operational standard continued with the arrival of Spitfires L1063, L1064, L1068, L1069, L1095, L1096, N3023, N3024 and N3025 by the end of the month. A move to Acklington was ordered, and completed on 7 October, to stand up for operational duty. Some scrambles were carried out, but the squadron was ordered to move yet again, this time to Drem on the 17th, and then to Kinloss, before returning to Drem. From then on, the squadron was kept busy carrying out patrols or scrambles (all uneventful) from Drem and Kinloss (where a one-week deployment was scheduled from time to time). This routine was maintained during the early weeks of 1940, by which time a new CO, S/L M.T. Avent, had taken over. Returning from a practice flight on 7

Winter 1939–1940 at Drem. In snowy weather, Spitfire L1008/PR-K is being prepared for its next flight.

Two 609 Sqn Spitfires during the Phoney War. Above, L1068/PR-B (note the serial painted on the fin and the undersurfaces with White/Night for the wings and aluminium fuselage and elevator); below, N3024/PR-H.

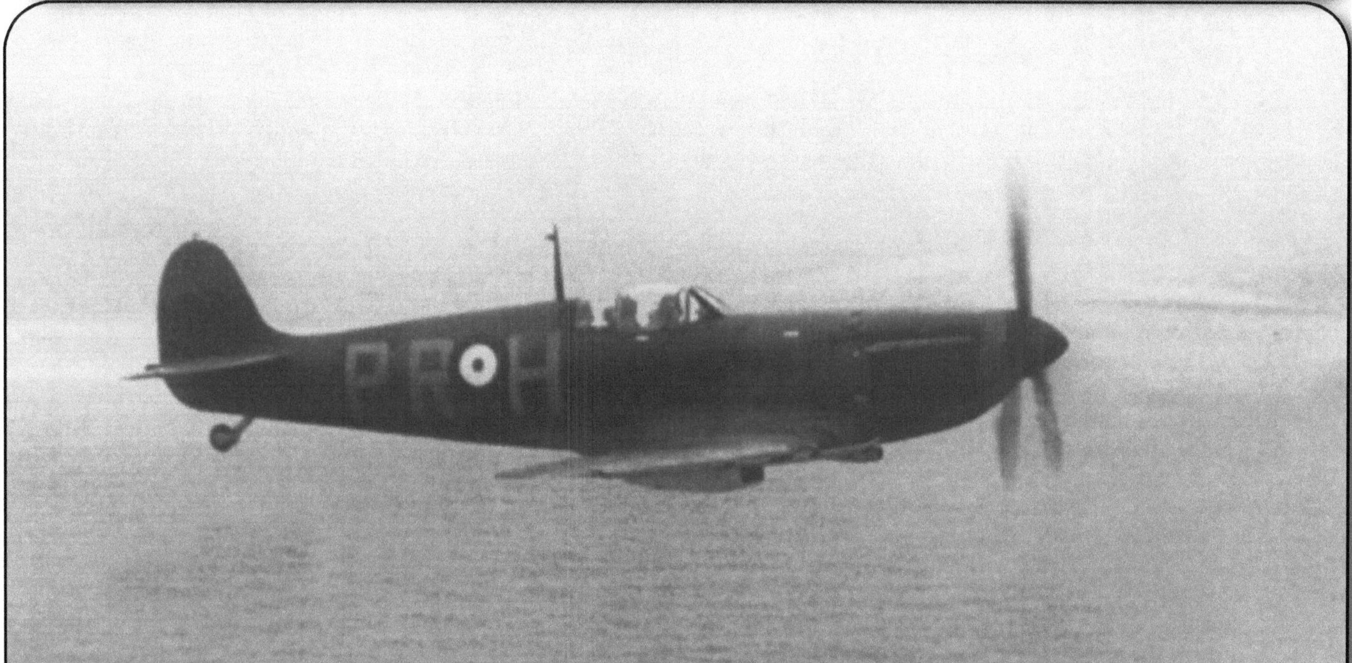

Two 609 Sqn Spitfires at Drem ready to taxi out for another patrol, 'PR-O' leading. Note the black underside markings on the port wing. These were used up to June 1940.

January 1940, the undercarriage of L1064 jammed and only one wheel could be made to lower; Flying Officer I.B.N. Russell, an Australian serving in the RAF, chose to bale out and landed safely while the Spitfire crashed at Crook of Alves and burnt out on impact. On 29 January, while doing practice flying with circuits and landings, Red Section (F/L D. Persse-Joynt, an Irishman, F/O G.D. Ayre, a Newfoundlander, and F/O Edge) was ordered by Control to intercept an enemy aircraft bombing a trawler at mouth of the Tay. The enemy aircraft, an He111, was first seen flying at 15,000 feet a mile east of the Tay over a merchant ship which was engaging it with its AA guns. The attack was initiated from line astern and Persse-Joynt opened fire at 400 yards with a long burst of twelve seconds. The Heinkel climbed into cloud, replying with its guns without effect. Persse-Joynt broke away to allow Edge to fire a five-second burst from 350 yards; he then followed the bomber into clouds. The Heinkel re-appeared flying north-east and Edge fired another burst, this time of two seconds, on its quarter when the enemy aircraft was again lost in cloud. It re-appeared once more, flying east this time, and Edge fired the rest of his ammunition in a long burst, but no results were observed. By coincidence, it was learned in early May that the He111 did return to its base as the pilot was later shot down over Wick and volunteered this information. Flying Officer Ayre was not able to fly in the formation and did not take part of the action. While this first action failed to produce a definite result, the second resulted in success. On 27 February, while on a convoy patrol, a He111 was sighted by Persse-Joynt who was leading Ayre and P/O J.R. Buchanan. The Heinkel probably saw the Spitfires coming. It climbed into cloud and was followed by Persse-Joynt who then lost sight of the enemy aircraft. The He111 came back down through the cloud, however, and was seen by Ayre and Buchanan who each made two attacks, setting the bomber's engines on fire. The Heinkel went into the sea and the crew was seen to escape by rubber boat; they were soon taken prisoner. To shoot down the He111, Ayre fired 2560 rounds and Buchanan 2800, the latter returning to base with fourteen holes in his machine. This was the first confirmed claim made by 609. February had been busy with about 325 patrols carried out and this number was increased to close to 350 in March. While no further claims were made, the squadron lost a Spitfire when Ayre crashed on the 19th, overshooting his landing on return from a practice flight. The Spitfire was declared unrepairable on 13 May. In April, a further 250 sorties were flown but it was an extremely quiet month from the point of view of operational flying. The squadron took every opportunity to get the maximum amount of training in, particularly section dummy attacks on Blenheim fighters. Little night flying was performed because of the weather. May started as the other months had but, on the 10th, the Germans launched their offensive. The squadron was not engaged initially but flying intensified. On the 15th, F/O G. Proudman, while attached from No. 65 Squadron with his experimental 20mm cannon-equipped Spitfire, landed on top of another aircraft (L1085), writing off his rare Spitfire. On 18 May, 609 received orders to move to Tangmere; this was soon altered to Northolt. The move was completed on the 21st. There was little operational flying at first, but the aircraft received armour plates on 29 and 30 May, and uneventful patrols were carried out over Dunkirk on the 30th. Sadly, F/O Ayre was killed when he crashed after spinning in on approach for a forced landing after apparently running out of petrol.

The next few days were very busy and intense. On 31 May, the squadron received orders to rendezvous at North Weald at 12:30 and stand by at thirty minutes' availability. The evacuation of Dunkirk was well underway and protection of the withdrawing troops and vessels was paramount. The pilots did not have to wait too long as the first patrol was ordered with take-off at 13:45, the unit taking the top position of the formation at 20,000 feet. Only eight Spitfires could take part. They maintained their altitude until they spotted enemy aircraft below. Flight Lieutenant D. Persse-Joynt, accompanied by the two other pilots of his section, dived to 10,000 feet to investigate. They soon identified two He111s and F/O I.B.N. Russell attacked one of them, disabling an engine and claiming it as damaged, while P/O C.N. Overton climbed back to patrol altitude following an order from his flight CO. This was the last order given by Persse-Joynt as he was never seen again. Flying Officer J. Dawson met the second He111 and made two attacks on it. While there was no conclusive evidence, it appears he only damaged the bomber. The squadron flew nine Spitfires on a second patrol in the late afternoon. This time they were not given the top cover but close cover for Defiants of No. 264 Squadron at 10,000 feet. Immediately after arriving over Dunkirk, 609 was engaged. The German bombers could be seen bombing shipping which was responding with every AA gun available. The squadron attacked a formation of about fifteen He111s escorted by about twenty Bf109s. An He111 was destroyed by F/O Russell (who was leading) and together he and P/O Overton found a second He111, which had broken formation, and sent it into the sea in flames. Russell then went to the rescue to Sergeant G.C. Bennett who was under attack by Bf109s. Russell turned into a Bf109, firing from 100 yards with two rings' deflection. He saw his opponent lose six feet of its left wing and dive straight in. Bennett, however, was hit, and came down in the sea near Dover where he was picked up by a boat directed to him by Russell. Meanwhile, Overton got another Bf109, firing from 70 yards. The section led by F/O P. Drummond-Hay had, in the meantime, spotted other bombers. Drummond-Hay sealed the fate of a Do17 and may have been saved by P/O J.R. Buchanan, his No 3, who hit a Bf109 which was coming straight at Drummond-Hay. Buchanan could not finish off the Bf109 and switched to an apparently slightly damaged He111 flying 200 feet below him. After a full beam attack, the He111 jettisoned its bomb load and headed for the coast with one engine out of action and its undercarriage fully down. Buchanan had a heart-stopping moment when his own engine almost cut out; he was ready to make a forced landing when it picked up again. A wise decision led him to break off and return home, landing at Manston soon after. While Buchanan made it home, this was not the case for F/O J.C. Gilbert who was posted missing. At the same time, the section led by F/O F.J. Howell spotted a single Ju88 on its bombing run. Pilot Officers Dawson and J. Dundas attacked it, the bomber opening fire first but this soon ceased when Dawson, and then Dundas, attacked. They shared the claim. On 1 June, 609 was again called upon to help protect the evacuation. More than twenty sorties were flown over Dunkirk that day, but very little enemy activity was encountered. Two patrols were flown, one in the afternoon, the other in the evening. Some engagements were recorded, however, each time involving one section. On the first patrol, Flying Officers Edge and Russell were attacked by a Bf110 which shot down the latter. Edge saw Russell, surrounded by bursting shells and tracer, pull up in a near-vertical climb then fall off in a stall and commence a long, slow spiral into the sea. Edge followed him down, until it was obvious Russell was not in control, and then climbed hard. The Bf110 was still there flying a wide circle. Edge pulled his Spitfire round hard and tried a deflection shot but his nose swung violently off-target because the four guns in the right wing failed to fire. Despite this, Edge repeated his attack when, suddenly, the Bf110 turned sharply and attacked head-on. It seemed it was deliberately trying to ram the Spitfire and, with a closing speed of at least 400 mph, a collision seemed imminent as Edge continued firing. At the last second, he rammed the stick forward and avoided the Bf110 but the latter was mortally hit as it turned on its back and plunged vertically into the haze just above the sea. In the evening, F/O Howell and his section, Dundas and Dawson, was engaged. They encountered several Heinkel 111s, damaging two. Dawson was last seen attacking another one before the escorting Bf110s showed up, stopping the attack. It was presumed Dawson was shot down by the Bf110s. The next day, 609 returned over Dunkirk with a single, uneventful patrol by five Spitfires; the evacuation was effectively over anyway. The rest of the month was much quieter and the squadron was re-organised as new pilots arrived and older ones received promotions. Squadron Leader M.T. Avent also relinquished command to S/L Horace . Darley on the 28th. Now the squadron was prepared for the next battle...

June 1940 and 609 Sqn is now based at Northolt. L1065/PR-E waits at dispersal. New national markings have been introduced with the yellow ring around the roundel. Note the topside wing roundel is still of the older, smaller design.

Some interesting characters were already serving with 609 Sqn before the unit's engagement over Dunkirk.

Top left, F/O J.C. Dundas joined the Auxiliary with 609 in 1938. He was called up to full-time service in August 1939. He opened his score over Dunkirk and increased it during the Battle of Britain, at the end of which he had become a flight commander and a DFC recipient. He was posted missing off the Isle of Wight on 28 November after an engagement with Bf109s, during which the top German ace at the time, Major Helmut Wick, was shot down (probably by Dundas). Dundas's score at the time was sixteen confirmed victories (four shared), two probables and five damaged. A Bar to his DFC was received posthumously.

Top right, P/O C. N. Overton joined the RAF on a short service commission in January 1938. At the outbreak of war, he was serving at the School of Naval Co-operation but was soon posted to an operational unit, 17 Sqn, moving to 609 on November 1939. He participated in the Battle of Britain with 609 and, when he was rested in February 1941, he had become a flight commander. In December 1941, Overton returned to operations with 145 Sqn as a flight commander and went to the Middle East with the unit in February 1942, taking command in April. The squadron became the first Spitfire unit in the Western Desert that June. In August, he went to 239 Wing as Squadron Leader Flying, his last operational position; a DFC was awarded in October. At the end of the war his tally was six confirmed victories (one shared), one probable and two damaged.

Left, F/L F. J. Howell was a long serving RAF member when war broke out, having joined the RAF in 1937 on a short service commission. He joined 609 in November 1939 and, over Dunkirk, was a flight commander, a position he held throughout the Battle of Britain. He received a DFC in October and, in February 1941, was posted to command 118 Sqn. Just before leaving for the Far East at the end of 1941, a Bar to his DFC was added. He arrived at Singapore a few days before the Japanese invasion and was given command of 243 Sqn, flying Buffaloes. He made his last claim on 16 January 1942, over a Japanese fighter, to bring his total to ten confirmed victories (three shared), four probables (two shared) and three damaged. He was not able to flee Singapore before the island fell into Japanese hands and was subsequently captured. He spent the rest of the war as a POW.

Claims - 609 Squadron (Confirmed and Probable)

Date	Pilot	SN	Origin	Type	Serial	Code	Nb	Cat.
27.02.40	F/O George D. **Ayre**	AAF No. 90330	(NFL)/RAF	He111	**L1086**		0.5	C
	P/O James R. **Buchanan**	RAF No. 77033	RAF		**N3025**	PR-R	0.5	C
31.05.40	F/O Ian B.N. **Russell**	RAF No. 37869	(AUS)/RAF	He111	**L1058**	PR-J	1.0	C
	F/O Ian B.N. **Russell**	RAF No. 37869	(AUS)/RAF	He111	**L1058**	PR-J	0.5	C
	P/O Charles N. **Overton**	RAF No. 40639	RAF		**L1082**	PR-A	0.5	C
	F/O Ian B.N. **Russell**	RAF No. 37869	(AUS)/RAF	Bf109	**L1058**	PR-J	1.0	C
	P/O Charles N. **Overton**	RAF No. 40639	RAF	Bf109	**L1082**	PR-A	1.0	C
	F/O Peter **Drummond-Hay**	AAF No. 90321	RAF	Do17	**L1095**	PR-G	1.0	C
	P/O James R. **Buchanan**	RAF No. 77033	RAF	He111	**N3203**		1.0	C
	F/O John C. **Dundas**	AAF No. 90334	RAF	Do17	**L1096**		0.5	C
	F/O Joseph **Dawson**	AAF No. 90331	RAF		**L1065**		0.5	C
01.06.40	F/O Alexander R. **Edge**	AAF No. 90325	RAF	Bf110	**N3222**		1.0	C

Total: 9.0

Summary of the aircraft lost on Operations - 609 Squadron

Date	Pilot	S/N	Origin	Serial	Code	Fate
30.05.40	F/O George D. **Ayre**	AAF No. 90330	(NFL)/RAF	**L1086**		†
31.05.40	F/L Dudley **Persse-Joynt**	AAF No. 90322	(IRE)/RAF	**N3202**		†
	F/O John C. **Gilbert**	AAF No. 90327	RAF	**L1081**		†
	Sgt Geoffrey C. **Bennett**	RAF No. 740558	RAF	**L1087**		-
01.06.40	F/O Ian B.N. **Russell**	RAF No. 37869	(AUS)/RAF	**L1058**	PR-J	†
	F/O Joseph **Dawson**	AAF No. 90331	RAF	**N3222**		†

Total: 6

Date	Pilot	S/N	Origin	Serial	Code	Fate
07.01.40	F/O Ian B.N. **Russell**	RAF No. 37869	(AUS)/RAF	**L1064**		-
19.03.40	F/O George D. **Ayre**	AAF No. 90330	(NFL)/RAF	**N3025**	PR-R	-
15.05.50	P/O George V. **Proudman***	RAF No. 39947	RAF	**L1007****		-
	Ground collision	-	-	**L1085**	PR-M	-

Total: 4

*Attached from 65 Sqn
**20mm cannon equipped

Flying Officer I. B. N. Russell in L1058/PR-J preparing for the next sortie over Dunkirk. He was shot down and killed in this machine soon after.

Victories - confirmed or probable claims: 14.0

First operational sortie:
21.10.40
Last operational sortie:
30.06.40

Number of sorties: *ca.*900

Total aircraft written-off: 10

Aircraft lost on operations: 8
Aircraft lost in accidents: 2

Squadron code letters:
DW

COMMANDING OFFICERS

S/L Ian R. Parker	AAF No. 90335	RAF	...	31.12.39
S/L Alexander L. Franks (†)	RAF No. 26053	RAF	31.12.39	29.05.40
S/L Andrew T. Smith	AAF No. 90337	RAF	30.05.40	...

SQUADRON USAGE

Formed in February 1936 at Hooton Park as a day bomber unit of the Auxiliary Air Force, 610 squadron was initially equipped with Hawker Harts before being re-equipped with Hinds. On 1 January 1939, it was redesignated as a fighter unit but retained its Hinds in anticipation of receiving Boulton Paul Defiants. This never happened. Indeed, when war broke out, the squadron was under the command of S/L I.R. Parker and received Hawker Hurricanes. That was but for a short time, however, as, on 28 September, 610

Wittering, October 1939, and conversion to the Spitfire is underway. L1000/DW-M is taxiing out for another practice flight. *(Andrew Thomas)*

Two key 610 Sqn officers in the spring of 1940. Left, S/L A. L. Franks and and, right, F/L A.T. Smith. Both would be killed as OC of 610; Franks on 29 May over Dunkirk and Smith two months later on 25 July during the Battle of Britain.

soon received orders to transfer the Hurricanes to No. 605 Squadron prior to receiving Spitfires. The re-equipment started two days later with the arrival of the first Spitfires, the full allocation being within a couple of days. A few days later, the squadron completed a move to Wittering on 10 October. Training continued in the meantime and the unit was soon declared operational with the first sortie, a patrol over the aerodrome at 20,000 feet, flown on the 21st. From that point, the squadron was involved in intense flying training while conducting several patrols and a few scrambles, all of which proved uneventful.

However, on 16 December, L1074 was written off after being hit by L1008 at it taxied past. The last day of December also saw S/L Parker farewelled with his promotion to wing commander and posting to command RAF Digby. He was replaced by S/L A.L. Franks. While 1940 began with more operational flights carried out, the first few months remained quiet and consisted of uneventful convoy patrols and scrambles, with just a few minor accidents to break the routine.

The routine remained unchanged until 10 May 1940. That day, with the invasion of Belgium and the Netherlands, the squadron was ordered to move to Biggin Hill. The move was completed by the middle of the afternoon. The squadron flew various patrols over the next few days, mainly over Manston, but, on the 20th, the pilots began to patrol over the Channel, closing the French coast more and more often, and then patrolling Calais–Boulogne. On the evening of the 21st, 610 protected the coast and shipping against bombing attack. Late in the afternoon, fourteen twin-engine aircraft were spotted approaching from the east off Cap Gris-Nez. The squadron immediately positioned to make an attack from astern; Red Section went in first. The leader opened fire and one aircraft was shot down, while the other section did not follow as some pilots thought the aircraft were Blenheims and broke-off. The Red Section leader broke-off immediately when he realised his mistake, but it was too late for the No. 18 Squadron Blenheim (L9185/WV-N) whose crew of three fortunately survived. Visibility was very poor, which partly explains the mistake, but it was a tragic friendly fire accident. Patrols and scrambles continued without incident until the 27th when 610 moved to Gravesend to cover the withdrawal of British and French troops from Dunkirk. The first patrol over Dunkirk was carried out during the evening, the squadron flying at 18,000 feet. After 45 minutes, an He111 was spotted midway between Dunkirk and Furnes flying at 15,000 feet in an easterly direction. The section led by the CO dived to intercept it, but S/L Franks did not open fire and overtook the bomber on the starboard side to ensure it was an enemy aircraft; the traumatic experience of the 21st had made him extra cautious. As soon as the Heinkel 111 was correctly identified, Franks ordered the two other pilots of his section, F/O E.B.B. Smith and Sgt W.T. Medway, to conduct the attack. Smith fired all of his ammunition at the fuselage and right engine of the He111 and, when he broke-off the attack, the engine was emitting flames and black smoke. Medway continued the attack, firing a burst of about five seconds, while Yellow Section made its attack with some short bursts. When Blue Section dived to attack, however, the Heinkel was on its way down and they broke off. As only Smith seemed to have hit the bomber, he was credited with the victory. During that brief lapse of time, the German crew had time to signal they were under attack and a formation of Bf110s went to their rescue. When they arrived, it was too late for the Heinkel but a huge melée ensued. The Germans got their revenge by shooting down F/O A.R.J. Medcalf and Medway but 610 managed to claim three Bf110s in return, one each for the CO, F/L A.T. Smith and P/O P. Litchfield, and three more unconfirmed credited to the CO, Smith and F/O G.M.T. Kerr. Even though 610 had lost two pilots, the squadron returned with four German aircraft destroyed and three more probables, a good result for its first engagement. The tally could have been higher as, on return, several Ju87s and Ju88s were spotted and attacked but only Kerr managed to open fire; results were inconclusive as, with their fuel gauges reading low, 610 was obliged not to press home the attack, returning to base after an hour and 35 minutes in the air. Two uneventful patrols over Dunkirk were flown the next day. This was not the case on the 29th. The first patrol over Dunkirk was carried out mid-afternoon. The squadron was caught by Bf109s and, for its first engagement with Bf109s, the balance went to the British who claimed four destroyed, one each for S/L Franks, F/L J. Ellis, F/O G.L. Chambers and P/O S.C. Norris, but two pilots failed to return (F/O Kerr and F/O J. Kerr-Wilson). The squadron was back over Dunkirk that evening. They had only just arrived over the beaches at 12,000 feet when they were fired on by either Royal Navy ships or AA guns on shore. Sergeant P.D. Jenkins was immediately hit and baled out. He landed safely about two miles from a destroyer and his leader, F/L Ellis, who had followed him down, flew low over the destroyer towards the parachute to indicate Jenkins's position, but the only response he got was from the ship's Bofor guns. Jenkins was never seen again. His misadventure distracted the other pilots who didn't see that the CO was also missing, probably hit just after Jenkins. Franks's body later washed up on one of the small islands along the Dutch coast. His position was taken the following day by F/L Smith, one of the original Auxiliary officers. While he officially took command of the squadron, his lack of flying experience obliged him to initially leave leading the squadron on operations to Ellis. The

In the spring of 1940, some leading 610 Sqn pilots, like F/L J. Ellis (top left), began to emerge. He enlisted in the RAF for a short service commission and was serving with 213 Sqn when war broke out. Two weeks later, he was posted to 610 to command B Flight. By the end of July, he was put in command of 610 and a DFC was awarded the following month. He led the unit until the end of his tour in April 1941 and added a Bar to his DFC in May.

He volunteered to serve overseas and, at the end of 1941, went to the Middle East, but it was not until April 1943 that he returned to an operational unit when he became wing leader of the Krendi Wing on Malta. On 13 June 1943, he was posted missing over Sicily but was reported as a POW soon after. His final tally was fourteen confirmed victories (one shared), two probables and two damaged.

Stanley Norris was also a pre-war RAF pilot, serving with 66 Sqn, at the outbreak of war. He was then posted to 610 during September. He later took part in the Battle of Britain and was awarded the DFC in September 1940 while also rising to become a flight commander. In April 1941, he was rested and returned to operations in August 1941 as a flight commander with 485 (NZ) Squadron upon its formation. As with Ellis, he was sent overseas and took command of 126 Sqn on Malta in December 1941. He left 126 in April 1942 for another rest. He assumed command of 33 Sqn in the Western Desert in November 1942, remaining in the role until February 1943. Norris was eventually posted to India in August and the following month took command of 11 Sqn where he added a Bar to his DFC. He left the unit in March 1944 and served in the Far East until the end of the war with the rank of wing commander. His score was nine confirmed victories (one shared), two probables and four damaged.

latter then led 610 twice over Dunkirk on the 30th but no engagement occurred. He led the squadron again on the 31st for the only patrol of the day (between 16:00 and 18:15), the squadron flying at 20,000 feet. It was not long before German aircraft were sighted and the section led by Ellis attacked a formation of six Bf110s, two of which were claimed shot down, one by Ellis and one by P/O Litchfield, while the other sections stayed at 20,000 feet to cover the attack. They saw Bf109s coming from above and Graham Chambers was immediately shot down. Pilot Officer G. Keighley was also hit but managed to fly two-thirds of the way back across the Channel before his engine began to fail at 3000 feet and he baled out. He was luckily picked up by a trawler and made it safely to England. A final sortie over Dunkirk was carried out on 1 June, before calm resumed as 610 was relieved, patrols now carried out over Canterbury, Manston or Dover. Intrusions by German aircraft began became more frequent and, eventually, one successful interception was performed on 12 June, when Ellis and his wingman, Sgt S.J. Arnfield, attacked and shot down a He111 flying at 500 feet on a weather recce. While the Heinkel dived to sea level to escape, Arnfield delivered the first attack, followed by Ellis, both sealing the fate of the German bomber which crashed in the Thames estuary. After numerous defensive patrols, the squadron was called to undertake a recce over enemy territory to inspect aerodromes in the northern part of France on 25 June. Dieppe, Rouen, Poix, Abbeville and Berck-sur-Mer were seen occupied but 610 returned to base without incident. The next day, the squadron was called to patrol Calais, again without incident, the Luftwaffe was not looking for a fight at this stage of the war. On the 27th, the unit escorted Blenheims on an uneventful photographic recce over enemy territory (Ostende, Dunkirk, Saint-Omer, Boulogne and Berck-sur-Mer). The squadron returned twice over the occupied continent before the end of June, but nothing of importance occurred besides the death of newcomer Sgt R.W. Haines on the 29th during a training flight.

Date	Pilot	SN	Origin	Type	Serial	Code	Nb	Cat.
27.05.40	F/O Edward B. B. **Smith**	AAF No. 90340	RAF	He111	**L1010**	DW-D	1.0	C
	S/L Alexander L. **Franks**	RAF No. 26053	RAF	Bf110	**N3201**	DW-S	1.0	C
				Bf110			1.0	P
	F/L Ambrose T. **Smith**	RAF No. 72724	RAF	Bf110	**L1011**	DW-F	1.0	C
				Bf110			1.0	P
	P/O Peter **Lichtfield**	RAF No. 73461	RAF	Bf110	**N3274**		1.0	C
	F/O Gerald M.T. **Kerr**	AAF No. 90336	RAF	Bf110	**N3289**		1.0	P
29.05.40	S/L Alexander L. **Franks**	RAF No. 26053	RAF	Bf109	**P9452**	DW-T	1.0	C
	F/L John **Ellis**	RAF No. 37850	RAF	Bf109	**P9451**	DW-M	1.0	C
	F/O Graham L. **Chambers**	AAF No. 90343	RAF	Bf109	**N3274**		1.0	C
	P/O Stanley C. **Norris**	RAF No. 40561	RAF	Bf109	**L1010**	DW-D	1.0	C
31.05.40	F/L John **Ellis**	RAF No. 37850	RAF	Bf110	**P9451**	DW-M	1.0	C
	P/O Peter **Lichtfield**	RAF No. 73461	RAF	Bf110	**L1075**	DW-N	1.0	C
12.06.40	F/L John **Ellis**	RAF No. 37850	RAF	He111	**P9451**	DW-M	0.5	C
	Sgt Stanley J. **Arnfield**	RAF No. 564115	RAF		**P9495**	DW-K	0.5	C

Total: 14.0

Date	Pilot	S/N	Origin	Serial	Code	Fate
27.05.40	F/O Albert R.J. **Medcalf**	AAF No. 90339	RAF	**L1016**	DW-Q	†
	Sgt William T. **Medway**	RAF No. 740320	RAF	**L1003**		†
29.05.40	F/O Gerald M.T. **Kerr**	AAF No. 90336	RAF	**L1006**	DW-R	†
	F/O John **Kerr Wilson**	AAF No. 90338	RAF	**N3289**		†
	Sgt Peter D. **Jenkins**	RAF No. 740830	RAF	**L1062**	DW-K	†
	S/L Alexander L. **Franks**	RAF No. 26053	RAF	**N3177**	DW-T	†
31.05.40	F/O Graham L. **Chambers**	AAF No. 90343	RAF	**N3274**		†
	P/O Geoffrey **Keighley**	AAF No. 90677	RAF	**L1013**	DW-R	-

Total: 8

A well-known photograph showing a section of three 610 Sqn Spitfires in formation. This photo was taken on 26 June 1940. Leading is R6595/DW-O; on its right is P9502/DW-Q (not fully visible in this specific photograph, see next page); and, on its left, P9495/DW-K. Behind, six more 610's Spitfires are also flying on formation of three.

Summary of the aircraft lost by accident - 610 Squadron

Date	Pilot	S/N	Origin	Serial	Code	Fate
16.12.39	*Ground collision*	-	-	**L1074**		-
29.06.40	Sgt Ronald W. **HAINES**	RAF No. 742106	RAF	**P9498**		†

Total: 2

The three Spitfire mentioned on the previous page (R6595/DW-O, P9502/DW-Q and P9495/DW-K) flying in loose formation.
Below, 610 Squadron with nine Spitfires on patrol in close formation. Spitfire DW-D was P9503, DW-H was L1004 and DW-J was N3284.

Victories - confirmed or probable claims: 5.0

First operational sortie:
06.09.39
Last operational sortie:
30.06.40

Number of sorties: *ca.* **800**

Total aircraft written-off: 5

Aircraft lost on operations: 3
Aircraft lost in accidents: 2

Squadron code letters:
FY

COMMANDING OFFICERS

S/L G.L. PILKINGTON	AAF No. 90351	RAF	...	04.09.39
S/L James E. McComb	AAF No. 90352	RAF	04.09.39	...

SQUADRON USAGE

Equipped with Spitfires since May 1939, when war broke out 611 squadron was already at its war station, Duxford, for annual training normally due between 13 and 27 August. It had been called up for active duty before the end of this period. The OC was S/L G.L. Pilkington. Thirteen Spitfires, the peacetime allocation, were available but sixteen were planned plus five in immediate reserve. Unluckily, one was immediately lost the day before the declaration of war when Pilot Officer H.F. Leech was killed in a flying accident five miles south-west of Wattisham aerodrome. On 4 September, S/L Pilkington, temporarily returning to civilian life, relinquished command to the A Flight commander, F/L J.E. McComb.

The squadron's first action took place on the 6th when ten Spitfires took off on an air raid alarm which later proved false. September was therefore spent re-organising the squadron, on a materiel and personnel level, and training pilots, although a patrol of six Spitfires was mounted on the 12th and another one by three aircraft on the 29th. The squadron, by early October, was considered fully operational and moved to Digby, a move which was completed on the 10th. October proved quiet and 611 was airborne three times on patrols, on the 18th,

Thirty years old when war broke out, James McComb had already had a long career with the Auxiliary Air Force. He initially joined the AAF in 1934 with 607 Sqn, then transferred to 600 Sqn and eventually 611. In 1938, he became A Flight leader. Called up to full time service on 24 August, he took command of 611 on 4 September. He led the squadron, over Dunkirk and later during the Battle of Britain, until mid-October when he was posted out, a DFC being subsequently awarded. No further operational postings followed before the end of the war.

Spitfire K9999/FY-D at Digby in February 1940 while other Spitfires practise over the airfield. Note the serial painted on the fin.

21st and 27th, for a total of 24 sorties. November and December were also quiet, with 27 and 43 uneventful sorties carried out respectively. The flying hours for these three months were 223 for October, 147 for November and 154 for December.

In the first month of 1940, the squadron's routine consisted of training flights, as far as the weather allowed, and several scrambles and convoy patrols, all with nothing to report on return. In January, 236 hours were flown. The squadron also began to exchange its older Spitfires (K and L-series) for new ones (N-series), which were fitted with equipment more suitable for combat. Some accidents occurred during this period of time. On 10 January, Spitfire L1033 had an engine failure on take-off, but fortunately, both the pilot (F/L K.M. Stoddart) and aircraft survived the crash. The end of L1051 would be more dramatic, however, as the aircraft and pilot (Sgt A. Bruce) failed to return from a convoy patrol on 28 February. It was presumed Bruce was lost in worsening weather as the visibility had dropped to 75 yards with various layers of 10/10 cloud and he became separated from his two squadron-mates. The next day, P/O V.G. Penney tipped his Spitfire (L1052) on its nose, fortunately without major consequence to pilot or aircraft. The same kind of accident took place on 27 March and involved N3055 and Sgt A.S. Darling. The Spitfire required minor repairs and Darling escaped unhurt. That month, the number of hours increased significantly with close to 600 flown. In April, the squadron ended its first stay at Digby, six months after its arrival; the number of hours flown by the 10th exceeded 1800, 800 of them during the previous six weeks. At the same time, all convoy patrols were stopped in the sector until further notice, making a total of 680 sorties flown since the beginning of the war. The next operational flights took place on the 22nd when a section scrambled to intercept intruders at 26,000 feet; the Spitfires were unable to reach that height in time. Two more attempts were made on the 24th and 27th, again with no success. Later, on the night of the 27th, 611 suffered two flying accidents. Sergeant Stephen A. Levenson was caught and held in a searchlight beam near Grantham during a night exercise. He climbed to 8000 feet and tried to evade but could not. He was temporary blinded and entered a spin from which he was unable to recover. He then decided to bale out and landed safely, leaving Spitfire N3063 to its complete destruction. Soon after, F/O R.K. Crompton struck a ditch while taxiing N3072. The Spitfire was, however, repairable.

At the beginning of May, the squadron was mainly involved in night practice flying while, in the day, the pilots were called upon more and more to intercept intruders, six times by the 10th; clearly the Luftwaffe was becoming more active even though some interceptions proved to be of friendly aircraft. On 10 May, 611 was told of the German offensive on the Continent. All personnel were recalled from leave. On the 11th, a convoy patrol was flown, the first for a month. Besides a few uneventful scrambles or convoy patrols, nothing really happened until the 27th when the unit was tasked with protecting the evacuation from Dunkirk. Led by F/L K.M. Stoddart, eight Spitfires took off from Martlesham at 06:40 to patrol over Dunkirk, but no enemy aircraft were seen. On return, three aircraft stopped at Manston, two short of petrol and a third with engine trouble. That would be it for May regarding Dunkirk. Otherwise, 611 was called upon to intercept unidentified aircraft on the 30th and 31st but was recalled before reaching the target each time and on 1 June, the investigation the aircraft proved to be friendly. Just after 01:00 on 2 June, the squadron was ordered to prepare for operations over Dunkirk later that day. Led by the CO, 611 flew to Martlesham Heath to refuel after which the pilots took off at 07:05 and joined four other squadrons. Over Dunkirk, the formation consisted of five layers: at the top, No. 32 Squadron (Hurricane), below them, No. 66 Squadron (Spitfire), then No. 266 Squadron (Spitfire), then 611, and the lowest, No. 92 Squadron (Spitfire). At about 08:05, a formation of enemy bombers was spotted and attacked by 92 Squadron, while 611 engaged the escorting Bf109s. This unit's encounter with the enemy lasted twenty minutes, during which eight victories were claimed:

Some pilots from 611 Sqn during the winter of 1939–1940:
Kneeling: F/O R. K. Crompton (†02.06.40), F/L K. M. Stoddart, F/O W. J. Leather, and F/L A. J. Banham.
Standing: Flying Officers B. Heath and H. R. Hamilton (Canadian, †29.08.40 with 85 Sqn), Sgt A. E. Brown (on the wing), F/O S. H. Bazley (†02.03.41 with 266 Sqn), P/O C. H. Macfie, S/L J.E. McComb (CO), unknown, and Sergeants J. R. Mather (†27.10.40 with 66 Sqn) and H. S. Sadler (†05.02.41).
Top, standing: Pilot Officers M. P. Brown and P/O D. H. Watkins (later OC 611 Sqn).

one Ju87 destroyed, two more unconfirmed, one Bf109 and one Bf110 unconfirmed, and three Bf109s damaged. The only confirmed kill went to P/O C.H. MacFie, who spotted six Ju87s escorted by Bf109s. He attacked the rearmost Stuka, which broke formation, and followed it into a pillar of smoke over Dunkirk. He spotted it again attacking shipping off the town and hit it during its pull-out, firing a burst from dead astern and then with a deflection burst as the Ju87 pulled into a climbing turn; the nose dropped and the Stuka hit the water, breaking up as it did so. The Germans took their toll too, F/O R.K. Crompton and P/O T.D. Little were posted missing on return. Five other Spitfires returned with various degrees of damage, while S/L J.E. McComb, the CO, nosed over while taxiing on soft ground at North Weald to refuel. The next action took place three nights later, when the squadron tried to intercept a German night raid, but no contact was made. From that day, air raid warnings would become a nightly occurrence and Spitfires scrambled (even though the Spitfire was widely regarded as not suitable for night flying because the exhaust flames blinded the pilot), but 611 did not have any luck in finding the raiders. In June, the squadron recorded 275 flight hours, a figure well under May (444 hours). While the Battle of Britain was about to begin, 611 had gained some experience, especially on operational flights with about 800 sorties flown, but had been involved in just one major combat with unimpressive results (one confirmed against two losses). On paper, the squadron was among the less prepared Spitfire units about to face the Luftwaffe over the Channel.

Date	Pilot	SN	Origin	Type	Serial	Code	Nb	Cat.
02.06.40	P/O Colin H. **Macfie**	AAF No. 90657	RAF	Ju87	**N3060**		1.0	C
	S/L James E. **McComb**	AAF No. 90352	RAF	Bf109	**N3058**		1.0	P
	P/O Denis A. **Adams**	AAF No. 90537	RAF	Ju87	**N3066**		1.0	P
	F/O Barrie **Heath**	AAF No. 90818	RAF	Ju87	**N3061**		1.0	P
	F/Sgt Herbert S. **Sadler**	RAF No. 565964	RAF	Bf110	**N3072**		1.0	P

Total: 5.0

Summary of the aircraft lost on Operations - 611 Squadron

Date	Pilot	S/N	Origin	Serial	Code	Fate
28.02.40	Sgt Alfred E.A. **Bruce**	RAF No. 740984	RAF	**L1051**		†
02.06.40	P/O Thomas D. **Little**	AAF No. 90364	RAF	**N3055**		†
	F/O Ralph K. **Crompton**	AAF No. 90361	RAF	**N3064**		†

Total: 3

Summary of the aircraft lost by accident - 611 Squadron

Date	Pilot	S/N	Origin	Serial	Code	Fate
02.09.39	P/O Henry F. **Leech**	AAF No. 90469	RAF	**K9985**	FY-G	†
27.04.40	Sgt Stephen A. **Levenson**	RAF No. 745292	RAF	**N3063**		-

Total: 2

between **October 1939** & **June 1940**

Victories - confirmed or probable claims: 9.0

First operational sortie:
12.01.40
Last operational sortie:
30.06.40

Number of sorties: *ca.* **850**

Total aircraft written-off: 6

Aircraft lost on operations: 6
Aircraft lost in accidents: -

Squadron code letters:
QJ

COMMANDING OFFICERS				
S/L Henry E.H. Pelham-Cinton-Hope		RAF	...	19.09.39
S/L Walter K. Beisiegel	RAF No. 26025	RAF	19.09.39	01.05.40
S/L Marcus Robinson	AAF No. 90161	RAF	01.05.40	...

SQUADRON USAGE

This unit was the last Auxiliary squadron to be formed, on 1 November 1938, as a bomber squadron. In June 1939, it was transferred to Fighter Command, initially with one flight of Gloster Gauntlets and one of Fairey Battles. On 19 September, shortly after war broke out, the squadron was placed under the command of S/L W.K. Beisiegel; he replaced S/L H. Pelham-Clinton-Hope, The Earl of Lincoln who had been in command since formation. During the month, 616 received a complement of pilots and, in October, moved to its wartime station of Leconfield, even though still non-operational. At the end of the month, the first Spitfires arrived, ten of the eleven being handed over by 66 Squadron. Close to 290 hours of training were logged in November and 270 more were flown in December. Declared operational in January 1940, 616 began patrols over the east coast and took up readiness duties. In all, 42 convoy patrols were carried out in January and 147 in February. On 21 February, while on convoy patrol, F/L A.N. Wilson, the B Flight CO, was leading a section as it descended through mist to locate a convoy; he was not seen again, becoming the squadron's first war casualty. The same day, another tragic event occurred when Yellow Section, led by F/O J.S. Bell, scrambled. Bell had to avoid a Battle just before he got airborne and struck a Miles Magister flown by a pilot from

Spitfire L1055/QJ-U at readiness at Leconfield in April 1940. If the undersurfaces, wings and elevators are clearly painted in Night, the fuselage seems to have been left unpainted as QJ-N on its right. *(Andrew Thomas)*

Two 616 Sqn pilots who made claims over Dunkirk.
Left, 'Ken' Holden joined 616 in early 1939. He was almost thirty years old. Called up in September 1939, he initially completed his training and converted to Spitfires. He was back with 616 in January 1940. He participated in the Battle of Britain with the squadron, becoming A Flight CO in November. He was given command of 610 Sqn in May 1941 and was awarded the DFC in July 1941. Tour-expired, he was posted away in November 1941 and would not return to operations due to his age. He was credited with six confirmed victories (one shared), one unconfirmed and five damaged. Kenneth Holden had a younger brother, Eustace, who also fought during the Battle of Britain with 501 Sqn.
Roy Marples, right, was not an Auxiliary officer, but joined the RAF in January 1938 and, once his training was completed, joined 19 Sqn in October 1938. When war broke out, he was posted to 610 Sqn in September 1939, to help bring the unit to a wartime standard, and was then posted to 616 in December for the same reason. Marples participated in the Battle of Britain until 26 August when he was shot down and injured. He returned to operations in November. In July 1941, he was posted to 41 Sqn as a flight commander and was eventually rested in October with a DFC. Posted to the Middle East, Marples joined 127 Sqn in June 1942 as a flight commander and was given command of 238 Sqn in July, then 145 Sqn in November. A Bar to his DFC was awarded in January 1943 before he was rested once more. Back in the UK, he returned to ops in April 1944 when he became wing leader of 145 Wing. His command was tragically brief, however, as he was killed in a mid-air collision on 26 April. His score was seven confirmed victories (five shared), five probables or unconfirmed, and three damaged.

No. 234 Squadron. Pilot Officer D.W. Coysh was killed but Bell was lucky to escape injury as the Spitfire was declared beyond economical repair three weeks later. The next day, Wilson was replaced by F/L D.E. Gillam. In March, the number of operational flights exceeded 300 sorties but another Spitfire was lost on the 5th when P/O H.K. Laycock's Spitfire suffered an engine failure at 700 feet just after take-off. Returning to Leconfield, the Spitfire was damaged on landing, leading to its removal soon after. The routine continued without major incident until 27 May when the squadron was sent south for action over Dunkirk, taking over patrol duty from No. 74 Squadron at Rochford. The first patrol of twelve Spitfires was flown late in the evening and was led by S/L M. Robinson who had assumed command on 1 May. The patrol lasted between 20:22 and 21:34 and was uneventful. The next day, 616 patrolled in conjunction of Nos 19 and 65 Squadrons, S/L Cooke of 65 Squadron leading the wing. On reaching the patrol position, two unidentified aircraft were seen and the Spitfires positioned to attack. In approaching the enemy aircraft, the squadron identified two Stukas; by now 616 had become separated from the rest of the formation. It was not long before Red and Yellow Sections were attacked by Bf109s; no less than thirty were counted. A fierce dogfight followed which ended with claims made by P/O K. Holden, who saw his opponent spinning out of control (one Bf109 destroyed), P/O G.E. Moberly, who fired from 200 yards' range and saw the Bf109's right wing break off (one Bf109 destroyed), and P/O E.W.S. Scott, an Australian serving in the RAF, who had come to the aid of his leader, Moberly, by firing a short burst at an attacking Bf109. He saw the Bf109 roll on to its back with blue smoke pouring from the left wing; the Bf109 remained unconfirmed. The squadron did not escape unscathed as the CO returned to base with a disabled Spitfire, Sgt Gidly was injured in the head and his aircraft badly damaged, and Moberly's Spitfire was also damaged. Flying Officer R.O. Hellyer was shot down but was rescued and returned safely the next day. The squadron returned to Dunkirk mid-afternoon, then late in the afternoon and in the early evening, but no action was reported. In the early hours of the 29th, 616 was again patrolling near Dunkirk, uneventfully, repeating the effort that afternoon. Three more patrols were flown on the 30th. Despite the lack of action, 616 lost the Spitfire flown by F/L D.E. Gillam when, returning from a weather test, he encountered issues with the undercarriage, the aircraft landing on one leg which collapsed almost immediately. The Spitfire was not seriously damaged but would not be available before the end of the deployment at Rochford. On 31 May, two offensive patrols were flown with ten Spitfires each (04:37 and 09:54); all aircraft returned safely with nothing to report. For 616, the next day started at 05:00 with a patrol by ten aircraft to protect shipping evacuating troops from Dunkirk. One Dornier 17 was seen bombing shipping; it was escorted by Bf109s which were engaged. However, cloud and poor visibility helped the Germans in their escape. The CO fired three bursts at a Bf109 before it disappeared into cloud and F/O E.F. St. Aubyn fired at another before it was also lost in cloud. Pilot Officer Holden had more luck. As he was approaching Dunkirk at 2000 feet, he saw two Bf109s circling warships. He gave chase, firing a long burst at one. Small flames came from the engine as the aircraft rolled onto its back and dove into cloud. The Bf109 was claimed as destroyed. Holden forgot to check his petrol gauge and was lucky to make it home, short of petrol, where he crash-landed. Flying Officer Bell was also fortunate as, while he claimed one Bf109 destroyed, he was shot down into the sea where, he later stated, he was machine-gunned by other German pilots. He survived and was evacuated by ship the same day without a scratch. At 08:25, F/L Gillam led the patrol with Nos 19, 41 and 222 Squadrons. They engaged numerous unescorted enemy bombers of all types that were bombing shipping off Dunkirk. Gillam damaged one Ju88, as did P/O D.S. Smith, while P/O H.K. Laycock damaged an He111. Despite his efforts, P/O R. Marples fired all of his ammunition at five He111s from close range, causing considerable damage to one of them but nothing more. Moberly did better by claiming one Ju88 after shooting off its tail. Sergeant Percy Copeland claimed an He111 as possibly destroyed; after it was hit, it stalled and exploded but its destruction could not be confirmed. It was a good day for 616. The squadron returned over the area once again in the early hours, but no action followed and, in the afternoon, five Spitfires scrambled to intercept an 'X' raid but they returned without anything to report. On 3 June, a heavy mist prevented any patrols before 06:00. Then ten Spitfires, led by the CO, took off for a patrol until 07:15. No enemy aircraft were encountered. The next day, the same weather conditions returned, but the importance of carrying out such patrols as the evacuation neared its end led to nine aircraft setting out at 04:17. The bad visibility caused the death of P/O E.W.S Scott, the Australian who had saved

Moberly on 28 May, who crashed near Rochford shortly after take-off; the patrol was otherwise uneventful. The next day, the squadron was at readiness in the morning then, in the evening, eight Spitfires (the squadron's entire strength at the time!) were tasked with patrolling Rochford at 3000 feet in the hope of intercepting another 'X' raid that didn't come. This was the unit's last effort from Rochford, as 74 Squadron returned to relieve 616 so the latter could return to Leconfield where it continued its standard patrols until the end of the month. During one such patrol on 19 June, John Bell encountered an He115 marauding near Hull at 10,000 feet. He attacked the Heinkel as it dived to 200 feet, jettisoned its bombs and headed out to sea with smoke issuing from the tail. On return to base, Bell claimed the He1115 as unconfirmed. It wouldn't be the last claim before the Battle of Britain as Roy Marples encountered a He111 near Hornsea at 15,000 feet in the early hours of the 29th. He attacked the Heinkel with two short bursts. Marples noticed return fire stopped after the first burst and smoke soon began pouring from the Heinkel. Later, a crew from a Heinkel was picked up off the coast. They were possibly from Marples's victim but, as they said they had been attacked by a twin-engine aircraft, his claim was filed as unconfirmed. June ended with Blue Section scrambling at 19:38 to patrol base; they landed at 20:25. No enemy aircraft were encountered. Since January 1940, 616 Squadron had been very active, with close to 850 sorties flown, allowing the pilots to gain a lot of experience that would prove useful in the next few weeks with the first stage of the Battle of Britain about to begin. The squadron was ready…

Claims - 616 Squadron (Confirmed and Probable)

Date	Pilot	SN	Origin	Type	Serial	Code	Nb	Cat.
28.05.40	P/O Kenneth **HOLDEN**	AAF No. 90705	RAF	Bf109			1.0	C
	P/O George E. **MOBERLY**	AAF No. 90332	RAF	Bf109			1.0	C
	P/O Eric W.S. **SCOTT**	RAF No. 40852	(AUS)/RAF	Bf109			1.0	P
01.06.40	P/O Kenneth **HOLDEN**	AAF No. 90705	RAF	Bf109			1.0	C
	F/O John S. **BELL**	AAF No. 90051	RAF	Bf109			1.0	C
	P/O George E. **MOBERLY**	AAF No. 90332	RAF	Ju88			1.0	C
	Sgt Percy **COPELAND**	RAF No. 108956	RAF	He111			1.0	P
19.06.40	F/O John S. **BELL**	AAF No. 90051	RAF	He115			1.0	P
29.06.40	P/O Roy **MARPLES**	RAF No. 70868	RAF	He111			1.0	P

Total: 9.0

Summary of the aircraft lost on Operations - 616 Squadron

Date	Pilot	S/N	Origin	Serial	Code	Fate
21.02.40	F/L Anthony N. **WILSON**	AAF No. 90300	RAF	**K9810**		†
	F/O John S. **BELL**	AAF No. 90051	RAF	**K9988**		-
05.03.40	P/O Herbert K. **LAYCOCK**	RAF No. 40925	RAF	**K9946**		-
28.05.40	F/O Richard O. **HELLYER**	AAF No. 90054	RAF	**K9804**	QJ-P	-
01.06.40	F/O John S. **BELL**	AAF No. 90051	RAF	**K9948**		-
04.06.40	P/O Eric W.S. **SCOTT**	RAF No. 40852	(AUS)/RAF	**N3130**	QJ-J	†

Total: 6

Squadron	Nb of sorties	Claims (C+P)	Op.Losses	Acc.
19*	720	36.0	7	2
41*	685	8.0	4	3
54*	1,130	42.0	8	3
65*	400	30.0	4	2
66*	1,300	15.33	5	4
72*	760	11.0	-	1
74*	760	31.0	11	1
92*	100	47.0	5	-
152*	60	1.0	1	5
222*	150	8.0	6	-
234*	60	-	-	-
238*	-	-	-	-
266*	100	4.0	2	2
602	1,300	4.25	5	2
603	n/k	4,75	5	4
609	1,300	9.0	6	4
610	900	14.0	8	2
611	800	5.0	3	2
616	850	9.0	6	-
Total	**+10,000**	**279,33**	**86**	**37**

**See SQUADRONS 62*

The wreckage of Heinkel He111H '1H+JA', of Stab KG26, shot down on 28.10.39 by Nos 602 and 603 Squadrons, one of the very first German aircraft destroyed by the Spitfire.
(Andrew Thomas)

Supermarine Spitfire Mk. I K9962
No. 602 (City of Glasgow) Squadron
Squadron Leader Andrew D. FARQUHAR
Drem (UK), early 1940

Supermarine Spitfire Mk. I N3105
No. 603 (City of Edinburgh) Squadron
Turnhouse (UK), June 1940

Supermarine Spitfire Mk. I L1068
No. 609 (West Riding) Squadron
Drem (UK), early 1940

Supermarine Spitfire Mk. I L1000
No. 610 (County of Chester) Squadron
Wittering (UK), autumn 1939

Supermarine Spitfire Mk. I R6595
No. 610 (County of Chester) Squadron
Gravesend (UK), June 1940

Supermarine Spitfire Mk. I K9999
No. 611 (West Lancashire) Squadron
Digby (UK), autumn 1939

Supermarine Spitfire Mk. I L1055
No. 616 (South Yorkshire) Squadron
Leconsfield (UK), April 1940

Early undersurfaces schemes 1939-1940

Scheme - Standard factory finish undersurface scheme of Aluminiun, Night and White used from 24 April 1939 to 11 June 1940.
Night and White under surfaces wings, fuselage and elevator Aluminium.
(L1068/PR-B)

Scheme - Official standard undersurface scheme from 27 April 1939 to 6 June 1940.
Equally divided Night and White undersurfaces.
(K9962/LO-A, K9999/FY-D, L1000/DW-M and partially L1055/QJ-U with fuselage left in Aluminium)

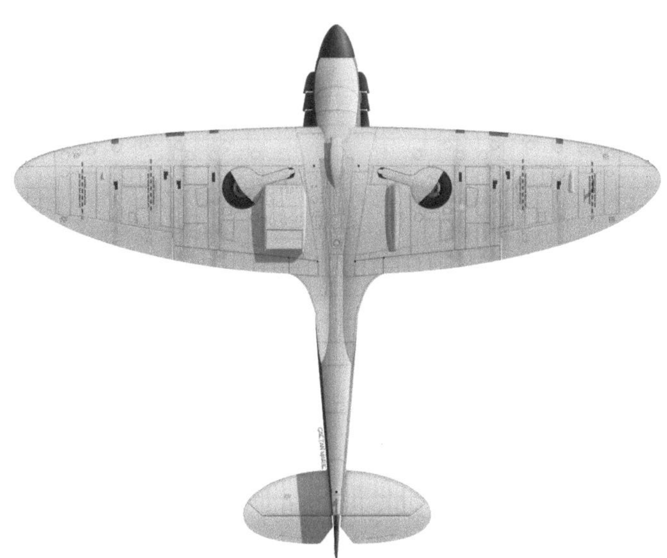

Scheme - Official standard undersurface scheme from 6 June 1940 and on production aircraft from 11 June 1940.
(N3105/XT-P with Sky and R6595/DW-O with Sky Blue)

SQUADRONS! - The series

Donald James Matthew BLAKESLEE DFC

Charles Cuthbertson LEARMONTH DFC*

Hans Anton MAURENBRECHER

Roland Prosper BEAMONT DSO* DFC*

Ronald Thomas SUSANS DSO DFC

James Henry LACEY DFM*

Introducing's RAF In Combat and Bravo Bravo Aviation's collection of highly-detailed and historically accurate, high-quality aviation prints.
For more information on available prints, please visit :

www.RAF-IN-COMBAT.com

or

Andrew Douglas FARQUHAR DFC

Prints available for this book:

PL-060: A.D. Farquhar
PL-153: J. Ellis
PL-154: J.E. McComb
PL-155: A.L. Franks